MEDITATIONS

It Is Always NOW!

MARDI LONG

Copyright © 2022 Mardi Long.

All rights reserved. No part of this book may be reproduced, stored, or transmitted by any means—whether auditory, graphic, mechanical, or electronic—without written permission of both publisher and author, except in the case of brief excerpts used in critical articles and reviews. Unauthorized reproduction of any part of this work is illegal and is punishable by law.

ISBN: 979-8-88640-346-6 (sc)
ISBN: 979-8-88640-347-3 (hc)
ISBN: 979-8-88640-348-0 (e)

Because of the dynamic nature of the Internet, any web addresses or links contained in this book may have changed since publication and may no longer be valid. The views expressed in this work are solely those of the author and do not necessarily reflect the views of the publisher, and the publisher hereby disclaims any responsibility for them.

One Galleria Blvd., Suite 1900, Metairie, LA 70001
1-888-421-2397

CONTENTS

Introduction v

01 – Setting the Stage 1

02 – Prepare for Action 7

03 – Act One: The Play Begins 14

04 – Act Two: The Rubber Hits The Road 20

05 – Act Three: Keeping It going 28

06 – Lessons Learned 33

References 45

INTRODUCTION

Mystic, mystical, meditation, mindfulness: What do all of these words, these concepts, have in common? After struggling and praying and studying, this book describes how it has all come together for me as a Christian.

It is about being aware that we are not complete beings if we do not reach for something outside of ourselves. It is about being curious enough to focus on these things and remain open to learning what lies behind them. It is my conclusion that a solid personal belief system that is founded in God provides the most coherent foundation. With that foundation we can begin to sort through the myriad of options and information that come rushing at us every day. As we continue to seek and find new concepts, we meditate on them and determine which pieces fit our belief system and strengthen it. We also will recognize and reject the ideas that undermine our belief system. This is the process that will give us fulfillment and peace.

One of the underlying messages of this book is to make a distinction between prayer and meditation. Why is that? **Prayer** is more about acknowledging our need for something beyond ourselves and **seeking** wisdom. The Lord's Prayer has been given to us so we will know how to approach this. **Meditation**, on the other hand, will be defined in this book as clearing our minds, opening our hearts, and then **waiting** as you ponder "the musings of my/your heart." **[VOICE]**[3] Psalm 19:14.

This allows time for all of the thoughts that are swirling in your head to come together in a meaningful way.

If you really do desire to get the most out of this two-way communication, both prayer and meditation, will become an essential part of your daily life. You will not want to live one day without it. Meditations may have words, or not. You may use the ones suggested here or, even better, you may want to write your own. By having multiple texts or venues that you use, you will lower the risk of this becoming rote. Sometimes it may be extemporaneous. Or done in complete silence.

The hardest part of meditation is "clearing your mind" of all that will interfere. It requires a consistent approach and lots and lots of practice. As with any pursuits for growth, be patient, do not be discouraged.

Seek the Sacred in the Ordinary

"The great lessons from the true mystics... is that the sacred is *in* the ordinary, that it is to be found in one's daily life, in one's neighbors, friends and family, in one's back yard."

Helen Mellicost quoted in *On Hundred Graces* - as quoted in *100 Ways to Keep Your Soul Alive*[6] by Frederic and Mary Ann Brussat.

01 Setting the Stage

THE QUESTION:

Why do Christians so often appear uncomfortable with the concept of meditation?

What the Bible Says

This question was on my mind while writing "Step 6" in *It Is Always NOW!* That is where I briefly touch on the topic of meditation. Somehow I sensed that this one word, this one concept might contain something valuable to a Christian seeking to find God. I realized that I did have some lingering suppositions. So I went to the Bible to see what I might find. Here is what I found.

First, the word "meditation" is not used very often. And all of those used are in the Old testament, all but one of those are in Psalms. Now, I did what I always do and used BibleGateway.com to examine these texts in several versions. One of my findings was that the older versions used the word "meditation" more frequently than the more recent versions. Here is just one example using Psalm 19:14.

King James Version [KJV][1]

> Let the words of my mouth, and the **meditation** of my heart, be <u>acceptable</u> in thy sight, O Lord, my strength, and my redeemer.

NOTE: For many the *King James Version* remains the "gold standard" version of the Bible. Although I once heard a minister say, "If you read the King James version and really understand it, you know a second language." Which speaks to the reason we have so many versions out there.

New International Version [NIV][2]

> May these words of my mouth and this **meditation** of my heart be <u>pleasing</u> in your sight, Lord, my Rock and my Redeemer.

Not much different. I have used this version for years in order to gain new insights. That is what I feel the different versions do for us. Just one word can spark a new thought. For example here, *acceptable* versus *pleasing*. Think about that for a minute.

The Voice [VOICE][3]

> May the words that come out of my mouth and **the musings of my heart** meet with Your gracious approval, O Eternal, my Rock, O Eternal, my Redeemer. Psalm 19:14

See what just happened? This version does not even use the word meditation – it defines it! I have latched onto this interpretation. It has clarified for me what meditation means for my own journey.

Just to be clear: This idea of different versions of the Bible is not new. Bible Gateway even has the *1599 Geneva Bible* (GNV). Then there are all of the languages the Bible has been translated into. Not to mention that they did not all start with the same version to translate from. Each one had to search for the right words in their language which would best convey the message. I strongly encourage you to do some searching of your own as you seek and find. For example, try this same exercise for the word "meditate" as opposed to "meditation." Lots more there to be found.

WHAT IS JOY?

First of all, the Joy here is not that giddy joy we feel as humans when we are thinking only of ourselves and get something "special" that we think we need. That kind of joy fades quickly and we immediately start seeking the next frivolous "thing" to make us giddy again.

These things are external to us and come and go like a day with the sun mostly hidden by clouds. The sun peeks out for a moment and disappears again. The real Joy, the real Sunshine is within us. It radiates out so others can see it.

This is what Jesus was talking about in John 6:35: "And Jesus said unto them, I am the bread of life: he that cometh to me shall never hunger; and he that believeth on me shall never thirst." **This is a "conscious and abiding satisfaction"** [Jamieson, Location 72233][4] or contentment that can only come from that special connection with our Creator.

BIG PICTURE

If you are seeking a truly meaningful and mindful understanding of life, it is essential that you learn to quiet your mind. It is then that you will be more open to receiving. It is then that the many thoughts that are swirling and churning around in your mind can come into focus in a meaningful way.

You must also study and reflect each day as you progress in your personal journey. As you do this, your foundation will grow and flourish. *It is Always NOW!* is designed to help you get started on this aspect of your journey. Now let me clarify "each day." For sure there will be days when you will not be able to dedicate as much time as you would like. What I find works best for me is to at least make time for my private morning prayer. Just that helps me get on the right trajectory. It helps assure that I have opened my heart and mind to that Connection and let the Joy in.

Here is another suggestion that may also help you. I have my Morning Prayer in a note on my phone. To make the practice of meditation work, we have to acknowledge the realities and complexities of our 21st century lives. One way is to take advantage of the technology at our fingertips. Be creative.

Clearing Your Mind

This is where the hard work comes in. Because of our communication overload existence, we tend to constantly be tuned in to receiving data and responding to it. That translates to quickly evaluating information without a lot of thought and never really taking the time to mindfully evaluate it. The idea that we might block all of that data and refrain from responding to it is foreign to us. So, this is a new skill we must learn. And learning involves practicing and failing and practicing and failing until we start failing less and finally start making progress. That is one of the big roadblocks. Often we are inclined to just give up in the face of failure.

Many books have been written on various methods for acquiring this skill. Here you will find some highlights which are only an introduction. Find the approach that works best for you. Try several. Do more research of your own. You might be surprised at what you find.

How to use It Is Always NOW!

AS A DEVOTIONAL

PRAY that your study will be meaningful and bring you new insights. Read each chapter in *It Is Always NOW!*

- Where there are Bible verses, go to BibleGateway.com and look these verses up in at least two different versions of the Bible. Or use hard copies of the Bible. Whatever works for you.
- Read the verses around each one to get the fuller meaning. Identify key words in the text of the book and the Bible verses.
- Use BibleGateway.com to search on these key words and see what other Bible references you can find that are related to the topic of the chapter you are studying.
- If you are using hard copies of the Bible and you have footnotes, these might lead you to other verses as well.
- **Do not study more than one chapter per day.**

WAIT. You need time to ponder what you found – time to let the thoughts that came to you come together in a more meaningful way. Some chapters may take several days depending on the time you have to study and how many thoughts might be swirling around in your mind.

WONDER WISELY! Do not rush this. Take your time. God is not in a hurry and you should not be either.

ADDED VALUE: You might want to create a document on your computer or have a physical notebook. Capture some of the thoughts from your study that mean the most to you.

Think Positively

"Traveler: 'What kind of weather are we going to have today?'"
"Shepherd: 'The kind of weather I like.'"
"Traveler: 'How do you know it will be the kind of weather you like?'"
"Shepherd: 'Having found out, sir, I cannot always get what I like, I have learned always to like what I get. So I am quite sure we will have the kind of weather I like.'"

Anthony De Mello, S.J., in *The Heart of the Enlightened* as quoted in *100 Ways to Keep Your Soul Alive*[6] #35

WHAT DO YOU THINK?

Is the Shepherd being "wise" or "pragmatic" or "defeatist"? Or do we not know enough about the shepherd's story to be certain?

02 Prepare for Action

THE PURPOSE OF IT ALL?

Based on my personal experience and years of study, this book is for those who want to get the most out of their personal journey. Every journey requires preparation. In this chapter we will concentrate on the things you can do to clear your mind so you can better focus.

"QUIET" YOUR MIND

How exactly can you do that? If your mind is filled with worries, you will not be able to concentrate for long. Those worries will swoop in and take you off track. It is like a bridge to nowhere. There are two bridges on the Rhone River in Avignon, France. One that goes out into the river for a little ways and just stops. The other goes clear across. For hundreds of years attempts were made at the first site to take a bridge across the river. Always, the middle failed. They finally had to accept this and build a new bridge at a different site – a new "pathway." If all of your attempts to quiet your mind are failing, perhaps it is time to find a new way of approaching this. Perhaps it is time to develop a new pathway.

But, Let's be real

Clearly, God expects us to take care of our responsibilities. He tells us: "Therefore do not worry about tomorrow tomorrow…Each day has enough trouble of its own." Matthew 6:34. **[NIV]**[2] After pondering this for a while, I now look at it this way.

First: You have to define "worry." For me it means "take action on" or "focus on" or "take care of" something. And it *must* be something you have personal control over.

Second: A written TO DO LIST is a very useful tool. You may want three sections: Today, This Week, Future. Items on these lists might include some actions such as call someone or pay a bill.

Third: Review and update the list often. Identify the things you have control over and that need to be taken care of today. Focus on and pray about the Today items. Personal confession: I still struggle with this and sometimes go days without looking at my list. This sometimes causes me to miss something important. Work-in-progress.

Fourth: Make plans for the rest of your items as much as you can – knowing that circumstances may change. Then take a deep breath and "plan" to "worry" about them when their time comes.

To further clarify the point, "worry" in this context is not about feelings such as apprehension, anxiety, consternation, etc. These are reactions that come from not having a plan. For example, perhaps there is a bill to pay, but no money to pay it. This may require additional items on the list: like talking to the lender, working extra hours, cutting out spending on things that really are not needed.

What this process will lead to if you make it a habit, is learning to plan ahead as much as possible so that when you get to the day of that "worry," you at least have a place to start. Sometimes there is no good answer and you have to make plans to deal with the consequences.

But, accepting the consequences and powering through them is also an important part of this process. By getting to the "root cause" of a certain problem, you can discover new ways to avoid this same "worry" and its consequences in the future.

TRY THIS: Make a special list of the things you truly have no control over. Meditate on putting them in a far corner of your mind. Then shred it and focus each day on what you do have control over.

Easy? *Of course not!* It takes determination, daily prayer, meditation, practice, and resolve to attain consistency. As you do this you will slowly build new habits/bridges/pathways in your mind and heart. It will be easier and easier to find and stick to each plan. Just know that however hard it is, however many times you fail and have to refocus - it is worth the effort!

FEELING THE NEED

Now you may be thinking, "Meditation sounds like a great idea. I think I will do that." Warning: This is like so many other things in our life. We set out to do something, really get into it for a while, then it just fades away. What makes us stay on course? You must feel the need!

When you are hungry, you "feel the need to eat" – so you eat and that "need" goes away for a while. Same with being thirsty (drinking water) or tired (getting sleep) and so on. Now these are built in needs. Your body lets you know! You do not have to put these things on your "to do" list.

This does not happen automatically for things like exercise or cleaning house or paying bills or starting each day in your secret garden. You have to make conscious efforts and develop "habits" for those things in order for them to become a consistent part of your routine. These are what I call "pathways" in my books. Now I think of these as little "trenches" where messages flow – kind of like water. (Remember, I am very visual.) You set out to build a new pathway, you dig out a little "dirt" for the new pathway and throw it into the old one. Over time, the old pathway or trench fills up and the new one becomes deeper and part of your normal routine.

Now let's take this little analogy a bit further. When you first set out to build a new pathway you need to know that you will fail. Sometimes quite often and quite miserably. Rather than get discouraged you must recognize that the old pathway still exists. It is not completely filled up yet. In fact, some pathways seem to never get completely filled up. That is why our journey is always a work in progress and why it needs to be a daily pursuit. This is why God never gives up on us. He knows this and He is very patient with us. That is also why we must never give up on ourselves. We must keep trying.

As you develop a consistent habit of starting each day by going to your secret garden (if only for a few minutes) and consciously opening the door of your heart to let the Joy come flooding in, you develop a "need" for it. You become more dependent on that Connection to help get you through your crazy day. You are developing a new pathway which slowly becomes part of your life. You start finding yourself really wanting to go to that secret garden. You have experienced the value of it. You can see (even feel) that new pathway getting deeper. You want more.

Then life happens. Pretty much every day. It is much easier for me now that I am retired. When you are young and working and have children, etc., you have to get very creative. Maybe while you are alone in the car driving to work you play some of your meditation music or listen to an inspirational audio book and, yes pray – eyes open, of course. But, let's be honest, you are always thinking of something on your way to work. So why not this?

Or maybe when you get out of the shower you wrap yourself in your towel and sit on the end of the tub. Reach out to God while the door is locked and before life comes crashing in – literally. Also remember, you can quickly reach out to God during the day. Eyes still open: "God, I am losing it here. Please flood me with a fresh supply of that Joy and peace that only comes from you." It is always time to reach out to God. It is always time to take a deep breath and try again. *It Is Always NOW!*

RESOURCES: DON'T STAY HOME ALONE

Humans need other humans. God intends for us to be part of a community. It is another way to reinforce and expand the things you are studying and learning in your secret garden.

Study groups and/or book clubs with others who are exploring the same things you are is one example. The internet can be a place to find these opportunities. For example, on Facebook you can literally search for "study groups about God." Check them out before joining. See what their page looks like. There are also blogs, podcasts, YouTube.com videos, and, of course, books. Remember to wonder wisely.

Sometimes you need to talk to someone in private about a specific, difficult issue. You realize that this is the best next step in your journey. You might feel comfortable confiding in a trusted friend. Someone who has met the same challenges that you are struggling with. Or it might be a religious leader like a spiritual leader or a therapist, This is not a sign of weakness! In fact, it can take a lot of courage. There have been a number of times in my own journey where I am not sure how I would have gotten through if it had not been for the right therapist. Pray about finding the support you need.

Let me share some of the things I discovered about therapists over the years of my experiences. At one point when my father was very ill, I was really his main support. My daughter wanted me to come to another state where she lived to have Thanksgiving with her family. I was torn. Now, my father did have people coming and going to take care of his physical needs. But, still I felt obligated to monitor and make sure he was really OK. On the other hand, my daughter's life was at a rather delicate point and I knew she needed my support as well.

The company I worked for had options for me to find therapists. I called and they suggested one. The person I was talking to mentioned that this therapist had a social work background as opposed to a psychology background. That surprised me, but I did not have time to keep looking, so I went to her. And she was perfect for that particular need! That is when I realized the importance of knowing the background of your therapist. They are human too and do have different perspectives. Do not be afraid to ask about their background. After all, you are about to rely on them to help you make important – possibly life changing – decisions.

Equally important is to think through what they are telling you. If they give you advice that you strongly feel is not right for you, think and pray about that carefully before you act on it. The most important thing of all is this. *Tell them everything!* They can only guide you in the best direction if they have the entire picture. This is true no matter who you turn to.

These are things I felt I needed to put this out there. People struggle with the whole idea of seeking help.

To repeat the most important point here: Seeking help is not a sign of weakness! In fact, it can take a lot of courage.

PREPARE FOR ACTION

Live In the Moment

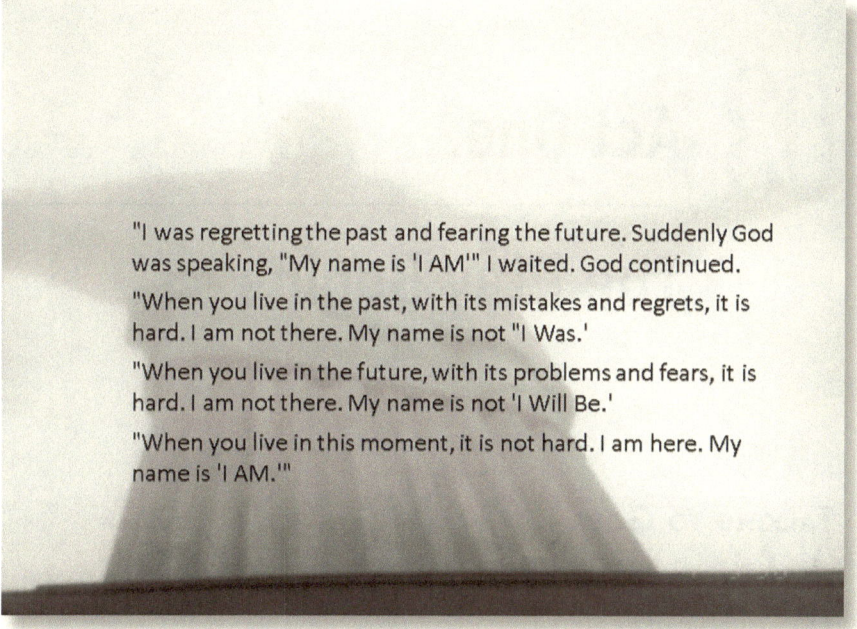

"I was regretting the past and fearing the future. Suddenly God was speaking, "My name is 'I AM'" I waited. God continued.

"When you live in the past, with its mistakes and regrets, it is hard. I am not there. My name is not "I Was.'

"When you live in the future, with its problems and fears, it is hard. I am not there. My name is not 'I Will Be.'

"When you live in this moment, it is not hard. I am here. My name is 'I AM.'"

Helen Mellicost quoted in *On Hundred Graces* - as quoted in *100 Ways to Keep Your Soul Alive*[6] by Frederic and Mary Ann Brussat.

03 Act One:

The Play Begins

TALKING TO GOD

God is our friend. So it only makes sense that we would talk to Him like we would a friend.

REMEMBER – FIRST YOU NEED TO SEEK

First, we must reach out and seek as we do in The Lord's Prayer which is always there for us. The following pages provide some *examples* of what your own prayers that you use in your meditation might look like. Use them if they work for you – do not hesitate to write your own. Or, just say what comes to your mind and heart, as you would with a friend. God is our friend. There is no one right way to reach out to Him.

There is no wrong way as long as you are honestly seeking. You may be angry or despondent. That is OK to express, too. God gave us feelings. He understands that at times our feelings run amok. Each time you pray you may be better able to focus on which approach will work best at that moment in your journey.

The Foundation: The Lord's Prayer
As interpreted by Mardi Long

Our Father, who is in heaven, Sacred be your name.	We acknowledge that He is God and give respect.
Your Kingdom come, Your will be done, On earth – as it is in Heaven.	We know that God's power is far beyond our own.
Give us today our daily bread.	Bread/food to eat as well as spiritual bread.
Forgive us As we forgive others.	If we harbor hatred in our heart, He cannot fully reach us. Hatred blocks the Joy.
Help us avoid temptation, Guide us away from evil.	We find the wisdom we need as we seek more of His love and open our hearts and minds to the Joy.
For yours is The Kingdom and the power and the glory forever	We acknowledge that He is the Alpha, the Omega, the Great I AM.
Amen	

See Matthew (6:9-13) and Luke (11:2-4)

MORNING PRAYER

GOOD MORNING GOD,

Here I am. You have given me another day. Thank you. Now I open my heart and mind and invite the Joy & Sunshine in.

I make so many mistakes! Yet, you never give up on me. Which is why I must never give up trying.

I pray that today – I may *keep that Connection* more of the time – that I will manage to not create too much interference. Interference that would prevent me from clearly hearing your voice.

I pray that today others will be able to get a glimpse of you shining through me.

Amen

> The light in the morning – Makes the path clear
> Open the Door!
> Your Secret Garden

Prayer for Any hour

Dear God in Heaven,

Thank You for granting me another day.
So often I take my eyes off of you and lose my way.
My pride causes me to make more than one bad choice.
Then, I can no longer clearly hear your voice.

Reinforce me with JOY that keeps me connected to YOU.
Fill me with HOPE that gives me strength and will renew.
Flood me with FAITH that keeps me focused and true.
Engulf me with PEACE that surpasses all that I ever knew.

Oh, You – The Great I AM:
My only source for that TRUTH which shall set me free…
Ever mold me into the person You created me to be!

Amen

> Never Alone
> Wonder Wisely
> Be Not Afraid

NOTE: This prayer has lines that rhyme. This way it is easier to memorize this prayer so you can use it no matter where you are or what you are doing. Kind of a "get out of jail free" card.

Evening Prayer

Dear God,

Well, I have managed to live through another day. I have made mistakes. I have failed to fully grasp opportunities that You handed to me. Take those now and make them as though they had never been.

Bless my family, my friends, all those who need Your love so much. Give me the strength and resolve to keep seeking and growing in You.

Cover me now in a cloak of Your Presence – Your joy. Take my brokenness and make it whole as only You can. Help me now rest and rejuvenate for another day.

Amen

> At peace with my soul
> Love! Judge Not!
> Transcend…

The purpose of meditation

After you ask someone a question – what do you do? Hopefully you give that person you are asking a chance to answer. Otherwise, why ask? It is the same with our communication with God. We pray as we should – as we must – as Jesus taught us to. Then we rush into our crazy, busy lives never fully realizing the answers. Most of the time we are surrounded by noise and confusion and a thousand voices so we cannot hear the answer. The internet, what we read, what we watch on TV, what others say to us, even a sermon in church. We tend to just start blocking it all out of self defense.

Now there are times when you are sitting with a friend on the patio and you just need to vent. To let it all out to someone you trust. To someone you know will not betray that trust. You might actually say, "I just need to vent!" It is OK to pray to God that way, too. But even then, do not just get up and run. Wait.

When you are on the radio, for example, you search for a station that makes you feel good or provides sound to cover up some of the confusion. Meditation is about just taking some time to let it all go. Tuning your heart and mind to receiving input. Input can mean bringing together the many thoughts and ideas – that are jumbled up in your mind – in a meaningful way. Also, to put your mind at peace so you will be open to receiving answers later: in something you read, something someone says to you, a thought that pops into your consciousness. When you least expect it.

Don't Wait to Start Meditations

Until your Foundation is complete. It will never be complete. This is a life-long, always in-progress journey.

Until you have your To Do List in perfect order. That is part of the journey. Seeking God's help in these matters is one of the purposes of meditations.

Until you understand it all. You never will in this life. In fact, the more you study, the more you will realize how little you do know.

Until your secret garden is perfect. That is most certainly not the point of the secret garden. It is not in the physical space. The secret garden is in your heart. The physical space is nice to have. But it is ambience – not substance.

Do Not Be Afraid!

Just start, no matter how unnatural it may feel. No matter where you think you are in your personal journey. What have you got to lose? Your secret garden, your inner self, is calling you.

Don't Try to See Through the Distances

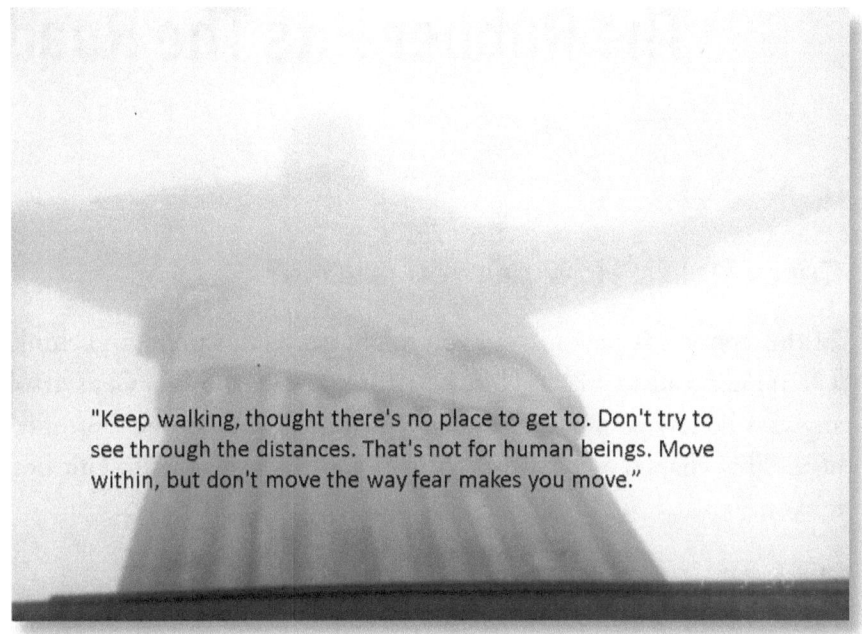

"Keep walking, thought there's no place to get to. Don't try to see through the distances. That's not for human beings. Move within, but don't move the way fear makes you move."

RUMI in *Unseen Rain, Quatrains of Rumi* as quoted in *100 Ways To Keep Your Soul Alive*[6] # 39.

04 Act Two:

The Rubber Hits The Road

CHECK POINT: HOW ARE YOU FEELING?

If this concept is new to you, you might get to this point and think, "I am not ready. I still feel like I do not know what to do. Get started anyway! Follow your own instincts. There really is no one "formula" here. This chapter is provided to help you find what will work best for you.

FIND YOUR SECRET GARDEN

- What is a secret garden? It can be any place that lets you be alone and focus.
- Maybe it is outside somewhere; In your own back yard or a park.
- Maybe it is a corner in your home.
- Maybe it is a walk on the beach, or in the park, or on a pathway.
- It might be for a few moments in a parking lot in your car.
- Even your car while driving to work. Have music you can play that provides you with some peace – that makes you feel more comfortable, more ready to face the day. An audio book that inspires you is also a good way to make good use of this time.

It can be different things at different times. It is about focusing and opening your heart and mind. This is the one, most important aspect: You need a place where it is quiet and your mind can wonder and wander. If five minutes is all you can get – take it. Obviously, more time is better. But life is not perfect. Don't use time as an excuse to not get started.

God is always there and *It Is Always NOW!*

Ambiance

There is no need to spend a lot of money or rearrange your life completely. But, if you are creating your secret garden in your home, carve out a space and make it special.

- A corner of your bedroom or dining room that you can use when the house is quiet.
- If you have a whole room set aside, add things that will make it more Zen or Feng Shui.
- Maybe a fish tank. Of course, then you must keep it clean!
- Plants. Real or silk. Again, the ambiance will suffer if you have plants that are dying.
- Art that speaks to you. Large or small.
- Maybe an accidental find at an outdoor market.
- Paint the room colors that are calming to you.

Things like art do not have to be expensive. Years ago I found a little picture that I just loved. It cost $5.00, but that did not matter. It made me happy to look at it. Later, when moving from California back to Oregon and sorting things out for the movers, I picked up that little picture and thought, I have so many "real" pieces of art – why should I drag this across the country? I put in the Goodwill pile. I still miss that little picture. Really!

Breathe

> *"When you own your breath,*
> *nobody can steal your peace."*
> *~Author Unknown*

Now I do not quite believe that changing how you breathe will alone change your life. But I am convinced that it is the place to start. It is part of the process. Most of us do not think about breathing, of course. It is something we just do. It is one of those things we do not have to think about. And that is a good thing. But, stop and think about it. Do you breathe lightly or heavily? Do you find yourself needing a deep breath now and then? Do you breathe through your mouth? Do you feel rested and ready to take on the world when you want up in the morning? If not, it may have to do with your breathing. These are things your doctor can help you evaluate.

Regular exercise is a great way to improve your breathing and your entire mental outlook. You need exercise! I do not care how young or old – if you just walk a mile or two a day or go to the gym and max . out. You will sleep better and think better and be more relaxed. Do what works for you – just do something! And stretches – I do believe in stretches. I have used Pilates bands for years and am convinced this is what keeps me moving.

The approach here includes expecting you to do your own research. This book is not about methods as much as motivation and general approaches. Anyone who understands me as a writer, will know that I am not into telling people what to do. Rather, I write to inspire and motivate: to open up curiosity, plant ideas and hope they will grow within you. There are many books and blogs and articles on the internet out there. Find some. Learn from them.

ACT TWO:

Letting it all go

It's the little things. Humans have the capacity to let the littlest thing bother them excessively. Some are more prone to this than others. It would seem that I am one of those. For example, I have a palm tree in my garden. I got it when it was just two feet tall. Each year I am amazed at how much it has grown and how lovely it is. I can see it from where I do much of my studying and writing. It makes me happy to look at it. It is my pride and joy. Did I just say pride? Yes, and that is part of the problem.

Then my gardener came to do his annual spring cleaning on my garden. He is wonderful and I am always pleased with his work. Well, almost always. This particular time he cut way too many fronds off of my palm tree – in my opinion. I was devastated. Every time I looked at my "precious" tree, I felt angry. I was obsessed. It took some time and prayer and meditation before I could let it all go. Just saying.

Of course, a few months later the tree had generated many new fonds and was starting to look lovely again. That is the way I thought it should look. You know, it is not easy being a human….

What You Might Say When Meditating

Example One:
"Clear my mind" [now your lungs are full of air], [wait just a bit], then, begin to let slowly the breath out
"Clear my heart" [now your lungs are empty]

Example Two:
Perhaps you have something you need to let go of – **anger** at a friend, **worry** about something you know you have not control of, **fear** of the unknown:

"Let the ____ go" [now your lungs are full of air], [wait just a bit], then, begin to let slowly the breath out
"God has got this" [now your lungs are empty]

Eventually you will find you can completely clear your mind and just receive the peace and Joy you need to face what life has in store for you as you walk out of the safety and comfort of your secret garden. If only for a few moments.

Physical Objects: A Few of My Favorite Things

First is a little medallion that I once found. It is actually a Christmas ornament. It is now in a lovely little tray in the drawer in my special corner. It is a representation of a picture my grandmother had hanging in her upstairs hall. An angle that is hovering over two children as they cross over a little bridge. That picture left a lasting impression on me. I found this ornament when my daughter was away for a year as an exchange student. Now I use it to remind me that God is always with us and our loved ones no matter where they are. Sometimes I touch it while I pray.

We also have a little plaque with the same image on it in the room in our home that is a space where our grandchildren can play or sleep when they visit. I hope that when they get older, they will remember it.

Second are some rosary beads. I found these in a little zipper bag when I was cleaning out my mother's things after she passed away. They are also in that drawer in my special corner. I find that moving my fingers slowly from one bead to the next helps me focus as I pray and meditate.

Then there is a medallion I bought that has an image of my favorite saint: St. John of the Cross. It is on a chain and I do sometimes wear it. I discovered this saint from a short reference our pastor once made to him. I have found his works online and they speak to me.

The idea of wearing it on a chain inside my clothes came from a Buddhist acquaintance. He showed me his Buddha that he always wears on a chain around his neck under this clothing. His mother gave it to him when he was young. It helps to remind me that he is never alone.

It's the Music

Music is another form of meditation that works for me. The right music speaks to the soul. I have a special set of music on my iPhone. When all is quiet, I lay on the sofa, put on my eye mask, put earbuds in both ears, turn the volume to a comfortable level, and just listen. As with words read on a printed page, each time I listen to the words in the songs may mean different things to me. It depends on where I am at that moment in my journey. It depends on what is happening to me.

Words are not necessary. The music may be songs you like without the words. My music happens to be religious. Soundscapes could work. There are apps like Calm that you can use. Try different things. Find what works for you. You may have several things that work. I find that changing things up helps to prevent rote, mindless meditation.

Journaling

This is a good way to capture what you are thinking. It is a good way to organize what you are thinking. It is a good way to evaluate and reevaluate what you are thinking. I once heard a group leader say that you must not use a computer. That allows you to change words which are not true to capturing your thoughts. I beg to differ. First, I cannot read my own writing much of the time. Second writing by hand does not begin to keep up with my thought flow. By the time I can get to the end of a thought I have lost part of it while focusing on writing the first part.

Since I have spent most of my career on the computer and I can type quite quickly, I find that typing my thoughts out on the computer is the best approach for me. In the end there is no one way. Try different things and do what works for you. It may be that different things work best for you at different times.

EVEN ELECTRONICS

Some years ago, a friend introduced me to a device called The MUSE. Now if you are not electronically inclined, this is probably not for you. But so many in our current world are, so I feel it is appropriate to mention it here. This is just one more tool that is available.

This link will tell you more: choosemuse.com
Here is a clip from the website re how it works:

HOW IT WORKS

Muse is a brain-sensing headband that uses recall-time biofeedback to help you refocus during the day and recover overnight.

Disclaimer: I am really not certain what all of that means – nor do I think I want to wear an electronic device day and night. However, l want to make you aware of it. What you do with this information is up to you.

ACT TWO:

GO INTO ALL FOUR ROOMS

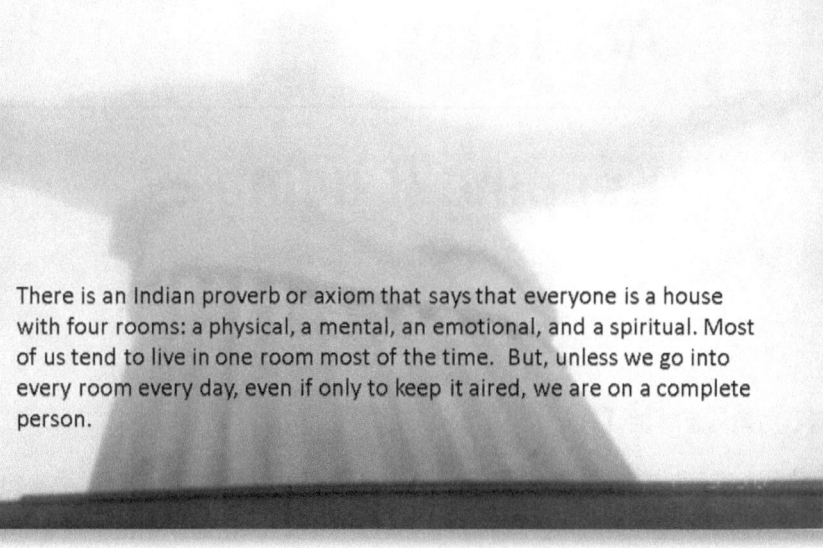

There is an Indian proverb or axiom that says that everyone is a house with four rooms: a physical, a mental, an emotional, and a spiritual. Most of us tend to live in one room most of the time. But, unless we go into every room every day, even if only to keep it aired, we are on a complete person.

Rumer Godden in A House with Four Rooms as quoted in 100 Ways to Keep Your Soul Alive[6] #2

NOTE: It has occurred to me that these rooms are not compartmentalized. Many times they blend together. Nor am I so sure we need all four every day. Still, unless we experience all four dimensions represented by these rooms on a regular basis, we cannot be complete people.

05 Act Three:
Keeping It going

KEEPING THE DOOR OPEN

Sounds good. Seems simple enough. And, yet, not so much. Life happens. The door gets slammed in our face. Remember, now is always the time to get back up and keep going. *It Is Always NOW!*

QUOTES[7]

"Sleep is the best meditation." – Dalai Lama [BREATHE p. 27]

"Strength does not come from physical capacity. It comes from an indomitable will." – Mahatma Gandhi [BREATHE p. 29]

"Change will not come if we wait for some other person or some other time. We are the ones we've been waiting for. We are the change that we seek." – Barack Obama [BREATHE p.60]

"We were designed and built to feel, and there is no thought, no state of mind, that is not also a feeling state." – Jeanette Winterson [BREATHE p. 71]

"To make people feel is the aim of art, therefore art for me is the science of freedom." – Joseph Beuys [BREATHE p. 86]

"Once the storm is over, you will not [may not] remember how you made it through, how you managed to survive. You won't even be sure, whether the storm is really over. But one thing is certain. When you come out of the storm, you won't be the same person who walked in. That's what this storm's all about." – Haruki Murakami, *Kafka on the Shore* [BREATHE p. 108]

Perspective

It comes down to perspective. Are we standing at the bottom of the stairs looking up? Wondering how steep, how uneven, how narrow the stairs are? Wondering if we shall stumble and fall? Or are we standing at the top of the stairs looking up? Knowing that you have conquered that passage and are filled with hope and desire and determination to continue on that journey?

Life is full of rough spots. Difficult times. Problems that seem insurmountable. But as we seek and find and grow, we become more and more confident and filled with the Joy that helps and allows and guides us to overcome.

Eyes Wide Open?

Perhaps you have heard it said that "the eyes are a window to the soul." Some say you really need to meditate with open eyes. Somewhere along my own journey, this aspect of meditation came to my attention. And I have given it thought and wondered and tried it.

One thing that has occurred to me is that if you ***can*** keep them open and still fully concentrate – fully block out all that is of the here and now – then open may be best.

In the beginning, when you are still learning to block it all out, I have concluded, based on my own experience, that closed is best. Only very recently have I found I can open my eyes. And it does add another dimension to the mastery of this practice. After all, our eyes are one of our senses. Looking up at the sky works best for me. You will discover what works best for you.

The Healing Process

When you get a cut on your finger, it heals one cell at a time. There is no way to rush it. You can hinder the healing process by letting it get dirt in it. You may be able to facilitate the healing process by putting Neosporin and/or a band aid on it to keep the dirt out.

It is the same with the healing of our soul. We can't rush it. But we can support and encourage it. We do this by maintaining our focus on God, by daily seeking the Joy, by sharing.

Conversely, we can hinder it by letting other things get in the way of our focus. Shutting down or creating too much interference. While we can lose that connection completely by constant neglect, God makes this very difficult for us to do!

Once we start on this path, we must not try to rush it. We must be careful to not blame ourselves when we fail. We are human. It happens. Now is always the time to get up, seek the Joy, and keep going. *It Is Always NOW!*

Is This Worth All of the Effort?

Oh, yes! I believe it is based on my own experience. Reaching up and out and letting go can mean the difference between walking out of the door with a heavy heart or with a hint of a smile on your face and a spark of hope in your heart.

ACT THREE:

Some days just go better than others. There is no changing that. But we must never quit trying or let that discourage us. We must never stop reaching for that "moment of happiness." We must always remember that we are not alone. We must always wonder wisely and enjoy the journey!

BE OPEN TO EPIPHANIES

An epiphany is a sudden realization of a significant truth, usually arising out of a commonplace event. At that special moment, a life meaning becomes clear to you - an insight into your personality, a discovery of something you value or believe in, an acute sense of where you are in life....Such moments can determine the course of your life as much as your response to a crisis.

Robert U. Akeret with Daniel Klein in *Family Tales, Family Wisdom* as quoted in *100 Ways to Keep your Soul Alive*[6] # 17

06 Lessons Learned

OTHERS HAVE BEEN THERE

There are times in everyone's journey when you feel alone or like a failure and you think it is only you. That is normal. That is being human. But, take heart. Here I share a few stories of others who failed and got back up or had epiphanies that helped them. You are not alone.

Now is always the time to get up and keep going. *It Is Always NOW!*

> **Your present circumstances don't determine where you can go.
> They merely determine where you start.**
>
> Nido Qubein

THOSE NEW PATHWAYS

As we seek and find more knowledge, our understanding grows. We see our life, the world around us, the people around us in a new light that lets us truly love and not judge. We are able to put things into a new and more robust and balanced perspective.

We all have those past experiences that we just "can't forgive!" We can't see a clear "pathway" that will allow us to look at this in any other way. That is human. Don't angst over it. Pray about it. God understands. Ask God to help you find a new perspective that will allow you to put this "road block," this "interference" that is holding you back – behind you. Even if you find it difficult to believe this is possible: You have nothing to lose and everything to gain by trying.

Personally, it took me years to forgive one particular individual in my life. Finally I had to accept that they were broken and unwilling to try and/or unable to fix it. But, why is it so very important for us to forgive those who do not want to change and have hurt us as a result of that? It is because not forgiving causes interference between us and God. These thoughts of unresolved angst will keep sweeping in and take us off course.

Jesus did not assume that everyone wants to get well. God will never force His way in. Here is an example from Jesus' ministry. See John 5:5-8 **[NIV]**[2]**:**

"Some time later, Jesus went up to Jerusalem for one of the Jewish festivals. [2] Now there is in Jerusalem near the Sheep Gate a pool, which in Aramaic is called Bethesda and which is surrounded by five covered colonnades. [3] Here a great number of disabled people used to lie—the blind, the lame, the paralyzed. [4-5] One who was there had been an invalid for thirty-eight years.

"⁶When Jesus saw him lying there and learned that he had been in this condition for a long time, **he [Jesus] asked him, 'Do you want to get well?'**

⁷"'Sir,' the invalid replied, 'I have no one to help me into the pool when the water is stirred. While I am trying to get in, someone else goes down ahead of me.'
[AKA: The man was trying.]

"⁸Then Jesus said to him, 'Get up! Pick up your mat and walk.' ⁹At once the man was cured; he picked up his mat and walked."

Does it sound strange to ask if someone wants to get healed? You see, they have to want something bad enough to work on it. Sometimes in order to be well it may require changes to diet and/or be necessary to get more exercise. Things that one may find onerous or difficult or frightening. Someone may not want to go to the doctor or a therapist. It takes courage. Especially to face things that have happened in the past that are buried deep inside and are very painful to think about. But those things do affect relationships with others, even if this is not recognized. These things can also affect how one sees themselves when looking into the mirror, and relationship with God.

Don't be afraid to get help. God did not create us to be alone.

In **Genesis 2:18 God Says:**

> ¹⁸It is not good for the man to be alone, so I will create a companion for him, a perfectly suited partner. [The **[VOICE]**³

Matthew 18:20
Jesus Says:

> ²⁰For when two or three gather together in My name, I am there in the midst of them.

A trusted friend may be able to help you put things into perspective. Especially if they have been down a similar path. Or a priest or pastor. There may be times when a therapist is the best answer. Do your homework when you choose a therapist. Research their background, maybe get a recommendation from others around you. But the one *most critical aspect* of this (no matter who you confide in) is to tell them *everything*! Hiding the worst of it will prevent them from being able to help you to the fullest extent. Pray and meditate on what they say as you go through this part of your journey.

Don't Get Mad at the Rooster!

Way back in my 20's I attended a Bible retreat. One of the speakers told her story about a rooster. It went something like this. When she was quite young, it was her job to feed the chickens. It was not so bad. She almost liked it, except for one thing – the rooster. He would come at her and peck at her. He scared her. And she would get so mad! Then, one day, God impressed on her that she should not get mad at the rooster. Or anything else.

That was not something I was ready to accept. After all, we have a right to our feelings. There are some things that we need to get mad about. If only I had listened – but, I did not – and that is now part of my personal story, my personal journey. Instead, like Moses, I spent 40 years "wondering around in the wilderness" of stress and frustration. Between a difficult marriage, a child to raise, and a demanding career, I found myself overwhelmed by it all. I was constantly reacting and seldom in control of any of it. My first response was often anger.

Yet, I clung to what I knew about God and never gave up. Eventually God did lead me out of that wilderness – and has given me a place "beside still waters" where I can breathe and think and find healing for my very soul. Now I share that story so that others who are in difficult situations will not give up.

Later, I had a friend who had come out of the drug scene in southern California. She was pretty much a mess. And she knew it. But she was letting God work His magic in her. She was letting the Joy in. She once said to me, "People look at me and say, 'That is a Christian?!' They have no idea what I would be like if I was not a Christian." God bless you, Kathy, wherever you are now.

Another time I was in a Sunday School class where we were discussing the "Tree of Life" and the "Tree of the Knowledge of Good and Evil." One of the class members said, "I may be way out on the end of a limb, but, at least I know I am in the right tree." I knew what she meant. I knew I was not alone.

But I want to go back to that rooster. Why is it so important to not get mad? What I finally – after all of those years – realize, is that anger causes interference between us and God. Anger puts us in a state of mind and heart that is not receptive to the still, small voice. Anger slams the door shut. If we really want to keep the door open, we have to be in a state of mind and heart that allows us to hear the still, small voice. *This is what meditation comes down to.*

THE STORY OF ELIJAH

There is the story of Elijah in I Kings 19. Be sure to read it when you get a chance. Long story short, the evil queen was after Elijah and wanted to kill him. Just as she had already done to so many others. So he ran. He ran and ran and ran until he collapsed in exhaustion. You see, God can not very well reach us when we are running either. So He patiently waited until Elijah could not run any more. Then he sent an angel to feed him and give him strength.

Elijah very much wanted to "see" God. So God used that opportunity to teach Elijah (and us if we will only listen) a lesson. There was wind, there was an earthquake, there was fire. God was not to be found in any of them. Finally there was a "gentle whisper." God was there. Do you see? The noise of anger and hatred and arguing blocks that whisper.

My dear reader, whoever you are, wherever you are on your personal journey: cling to what you know about God. Keep your mind and your heart open to that Joy – and never give up. We must persist! Read, study, pray and seek help wherever you can find it.

Once again, it is very important to remember that: God did not create us to walk alone. Yes, I am repeating myself because this is so important. There are times when you really need to seek help in your journey. When circumstances overwhelm and you feel you can't take another step. Seek that help. There have been a number of times in my life when, looking back, I am not sure I would have made it through in one piece except for a competent, caring therapist. Groups designed for specific life challenges like divorce or drug abuse can also facilitate healing. Knowing that others have the same challenges is very reassuring and their experiences can be enlightening and inspiring. It is not a sign of failure to seek help! God did not create us to walk alone.

THE END GAME

NOTE: I wrote this years ago when I was going through a personal struggle. No, call it a crisis. I needed to somehow find a way to put the turmoil that was my life into perspective. I can't tell you how many years that took because I do not remember. But it was years. I am just so thankful that I did not give up. And I still have to accept and live with the knowledge that there are many in my life who will never be able to understand why I did what I did. Nor would it do any good to try and explain it to them. But, God knows and I take comfort in that. Sometimes that is all we have got.

> The greatest ignominy [sorrow] of the human condition is that we learn too little, too late. And we do so much damage while learning it.
>
> The only antidote to this unfortunate state of affairs is to:
>
> Keep the JOY ever in our minds & hearts!! Only God can right the wrongs already facilitated and guide us in such a way as to avoid future ones.

Romans 8:28 [**VOICE**][3] We are confident that God is able to orchestrate everything to work toward something good *and beautiful* when we love Him and accept His invitation to live according to His plan.

WHAT DOES IT MEAN TO "TRANSCEND?"

- When you have learned what it means to open the door. When you know that God can help you reopen it when life slams the door shut in your face.
- When you have made it a habit of going to your Secret Garden.
- When you begin to understand what Hope and Faith are.
- When you are *working on* developing those New Pathways that allow you to want to forgive all and just Love.
- Then you can – if only for fleeting moments at a time – put aside that which is here and now and realize that Connection.
- The more often you "go there," the longer the periods of time.

Set No Limits! This is always a work-in-progress.
You will fail – don't wallow endlessly in self-pity – pray and wait.

To transcend is when you experience the Joy, the Sunshine – those moments of God-given happiness.

How to use *It Is Always NOW!* as a devotional

Pray that your study will be meaningful and bring you new insights. Read each chapter in *It Is Always NOW!*

- Where there are Bible verses, go to BibleGateway.com and look these verses up in at least two different versions of the Bible. Or use hard copies of the Bible. Whatever works for you.
- Read the verses around each one to get the fuller meaning. Identify key words in the text of the book and the Bible verses.
- Use BibleGateway.com to search on these key words and see what other Bible references you can find that are related to the topic of the chapter you are studying.
- If you are using hard copies of the Bible and you have footnotes, these might lead you to other verses as well.
- **Do not study more than one chapter per day**.

Wait. You need time to ponder what you found – time to let the thoughts that came to you come together in a more meaningful way. Some chapters may take several days depending on the time you have to study and how many thoughts might be swirling around in your mind.

Wonder wisely! Do not rush this. Take your time. God is not in a hurry and you should not be either.

Added Value: You might want to create a document on your computer or have a physical notebook. Capture some of the thoughts from your study that mean the most to you. If you are visual like me, you might want to use PowerPoint and add images that help you better absorb the insights you find.

Also, if you want to dig deeper, the Study Guide is there for you.

Hush My Soul

Hush my anxious soul,
For you truly have nowhere to go.
Except to the Light from above,
That wishes only to fill you with Love.

Hush my weary soul.
You surely by now must know:
If only you will seek that immortal Love,
Heaven will send its Peaceful Dove.

Be still my wandering soul.
Do not focus on that which is below.
Instead gaze ever with an upward turn.
Seek and find all there is to learn.

Look up and seek my frozen soul,
The Warm Winds that will ever blow.
If only you will open your mind –
Your heart's door – to the Eternal, always so kind.

Look up and find my fearful soul.
Focus now on what you already know.
Then go back again and again
To absorb Knowledge that will never end.

Focus and find my blessed soul,
The Peace that never needs to go.
Unless you let the demanding life in which you live,
Keep you from finding places that have much to give.

Focus and find my eternal soul:
That Power that will ever flow,
That Truth that will engulf you now,
That Beauty which will gently show you how.

**Life comes, Life goes – Life ebbs, Life flows…
See my YouTube video on this poem:**

https://www.youtube.com/watch?v=Ps2_7FyaNEw

Don't Make Comparisons

Everybody is unique.
Compare not yourself with anybody else
lest you spoil God's curriculum.

Baal Shem Tov as quoted in 100 Ways to Keep your Soul Alive[6] by Frederick and Mary Ann Brussat # 25

Closing Observation:

[Some] "...matters are so interior and spiritual as to baffle the powers of language." [St. John of the Cross][5]

Or as a Lutheran Priest once said to me: "We cannot reduce God to black words on a white page."

NOTE: St. John of the Cross was a Spanish Catholic priest who lived from 1542-1591. His mystical view of God and the Holy Spirit has been a great inspiration to me.

REFERENCES

1. **King James Version** **[KJV]**[1] Public Domain

2. **New International Version** **[NIV]**[2] Holy Bible, New International Version®, NIV® Copyright ©1973, 1978, 1984, 2011 by Biblica, Inc.® Used by permission. All rights reserved worldwide.

3. **The Voice** **[VOICE]**[3] The Voice Bible Copyright © 2012 Thomas Nelson, Inc. The Voice™ translation © 2012 Ecclesia Bible Society All rights reserved.

4. Commentary on the Whole Bible, Originally published: 1863, Kindle Version

5. *THE LIVING FLAME OF LOVE* by St. John of the Cross. Copyright 2012, Forgotten Books. First revised edition 1912.

6. *100 WAYS TO KEEP YOUR SOUL ALIVE* by Frederic and Mary Ann Brussat, 1994, Harper One, New York

7. Quotes from the magazine: *Breath and make time for yourself,* Issue 35, Published by GMC Publications Ltd. 86 High Street, Lewes, East Sussex BN7 1XN.

Visit Our Website & Blog:

There you will find information about our other books

MardiLongBooks.com
BLOG: MardiLong.com

www.ingramcontent.com/pod-product-compliance
Lightning Source LLC
LaVergne TN
LVHW041638070526
838199LV00052B/3445